VOT

D0441549

to
SAVE
the
PLANET

VOTE!
to
SAVE
the
PLANET

Jeff Schweitzer

3 1336 08001 0516

RVIVE BOOKS AND JACQUIE JORDAN INC.

A BURNING ISSUES BOOK

LOS ANGELES, CALIFORNIA, AND

WESTON, CONNECTICUT

To my wife Sally
For believing in me steadfastly in the face of
convincing contrary evidence

Published by
Rvive Books and Jacquie Jordan, Inc.
A Burning Issues Publication

Creative Management Partners, LLC
8 Gray's Farm Rd.
Weston, CT 06883

ISBN 10: 1-935073-00-1
ISBN 13: 978-1-935073-00-0

www.votetosavetheplanet.com

Printed in the United States of America

First Printing: October 2008

10 9 8 7 6 5 4 3 2 1

Book and cover design by Barbara Aronica-Buck

Acknowledgments Any author, whether accomplished or aspiring, knows that the publishing world defies logic. Nothing could prove that point more convincingly than the existence of this small volume. By all rights you should not be holding this in your hand. That you do, indeed is testimony to the amazing abilities of Jacquie Jordan and Darice Fisher, two whirlwinds of focused energy who defy easy description, and publisher-editor David Wilk of Rvive Books. With nothing more than a handshake and a shared commitment, Jacquie and Darice, as my producers, publicists, and media consultants, and David as publisher, worked relentlessly to bring *Vote! to Save the Planet* to life in electronic and printed form. These three people have done something thought impossible: they brought this book from concept to reality in less than twenty days.

Also indispensable to me were two friends, colleagues, and early supporters, Monique Raphael High and Ben W. Pesta. Ben was the first to take me seriously as an author, when nobody else did, and for that I will be forever grateful. Monique somehow was able to look at the manuscript of my first book and see past the rough language to recognize the potential for a real author to emerge. In our interconnected world, I certainly would have never had the opportunity to write this book if not for Monique's and Ben's early nurturing on other projects.

I am indebted to my wife, who tolerated my obsession on this book with her usual charm and optimism. Why or how she puts up with me remains a mystery, but I do not question too deeply for fear of upsetting whatever delicate balance makes such forbearance possible.

The 2008 presidential election is the background driving force for putting pen to paper, but I have been writing this book in my head for thirty years. Some family and friends would call that "talking to himself," but I choose to view my ranting and raving to an empty room as healthy preparation.

My political life began in 1972 with the presidential contest between Richard Nixon and George McGovern. I watched in dismay as the wrong person took the oath of office. McGovern was deeply flawed, and I disagreed with much of what he said, but he was infinitely better than Nixon. With the bright exception of Bill Clinton, my entire adult life has been dominated by the politics of the wrong person in office. Nixon started an ugly trend for me that accelerated over the past eight years.

The current race for the White House makes me tremble in fear for our republic. John McCain is Bush Lite compared to Sarah Palin. After two terms of abject failure, the country again is considering the election of an inexperienced zealot unwavering in the face of opposing facts because God is on her side. We would again have a (vice) president who disdains a "thick resume" and experience as liberal elitism. Have we learned nothing at all from the horrors of the Bush administration? Our country cannot endure four more years of a malignant presidency that relies on divine guidance in place of rationality, nor can the global environment endure another term of neglect and hostility.

Yet as the issues become ever more urgent, our political discourse has grown increasingly coarse and irrelevant. I only need mention "lipstick on a pig" to rest my case. We are fiddling while Rome burns. Human beings are fundamentally changing the chemistry of our atmosphere, but the media must focus instead on field dressing a moose. Enough. Enough. We are better than what we have become. I wrote this book because issues matter. I wrote this book to explore and encourage our better side.

Critics might decry my attacks on McCain and Palin as inconsistent with my hopes for a brighter future. Why not focus only on the positive? The choice before us is not between two equivalent teams in which our selection will result in something benign or good regardless. Explaining why Obama must be elected is not enough. We must also understand why McCain and Palin cannot be allowed to occupy the White House.

Consider a doctor trying to encourage an obese patient to go on a diet. She first describes the positives of losing weight, like easier breathing, better mobility, increased energy level, and improved sleep. But simply listing the benefits of a lean figure is insufficient; the patient must also grasp the grave dangers of his obesity as well. So the doctor discusses with him a greater risk for heart disease, stroke, diabetes, angina, high blood pressure, and heart attack. Just as the doctor must highlight the good and bad to explain fully the nature of the patient's condition, so must I. We strive to elect Obama not only for the tremendous good he will do, but because he will also prevent the calamity that would befall us if McCain and Palin were to be elected.

The election of 2008 is our chance to save our planet.

Why this book? Why Now?

All elections matter. Democracies depend on an engaged citizenry. We all know people who don't vote because they are alienated from society, or think their votes do not count, or are simply not engaged, lazy, or bored with life. If you do care about what happens to your future, your children's future, and the future health of the natural world in which we live, then it's up to you to convince your family, friends, and neighbors to take an interest in the election at hand—and more important, to take the time and energy required to get out of bed on November 4 and go vote.

Talk about the issues. There are many. Almost all of them are covered in this book and much more information is available on our website. Join discussion groups, either online or in your community. Tell everyone you know: THIS ELECTION MATTERS MORE THAN ANY ELECTION YOU HAVE EVER BEEN ALIVE FOR.

This book gives you a succinct and handy guide to all the issues that matter most. Use it to help talk and write about them in the days ahead. Get excited, get involved, make a difference. Every vote will count; not voting is a silence we cannot accept. No voter can afford to go unheard and uncounted, and none of us can afford to let the votes we need to get away—or to be taken away by fraud or subversion. Visit *www.votetosavetheplanet.com*

to join in an ongoing discussion with other people who care about the future of the planet.

After eight long years lost to an administration openly hostile to environmental protection, the fate of the planet may rest on the outcome of the November 2008 election. Humankind is destroying the resources on which all of us depend. We simply cannot afford to lose another four years. If this sounds alarmist or nothing but the hysterical cries of a tree hugger, consider the realities we face. More than half of our coral reefs are dead or dying. We have depleted 90 percent of all primary food stocks of fish in the oceans, including tuna, marlin, cod, and halibut. We are losing fifty thousand species each year, a sustained rate never before seen in nature. We are cutting or burning tropical forests at ever-accelerating rates. We are dumping 6 billion tons of carbon dioxide into the air every year. Climate change is not a left-wing conspiracy; it is a fact supported by twenty-five hundred scientists from 166 countries. The evidence is overwhelming. Polar ice is melting at accelerated rates; we will soon see for the first time in recorded history the North Pole free of any summer ice.

The environment matters in this election like never before. The Republican ticket represents old-school, outdated, and discredited views on the environment. But the environment is not the only issue that will determine our future and the quality of our lives. The problems we face over the next four years and beyond extend to other critical areas, including national security, separation of church and state, family values, and a woman's right to choose. Here, as with the environment, the McCain-Palin ticket is out of touch. Palin's views on abortion and rape victims are extreme even within the anti-abortion movement.

John McCain and Sarah Palin are the wrong people at the wrong place at the wrong time in human history. The two together would create a tsunami of environmental destruction when we desperately need leaders attuned to the urgency of resource protection. Instead, the Republican ticket offers us tired platitudes about off-shore drilling. McCain has chosen a running mate who is blatantly anti-science, which explains her sad denials about global warming, her ignorance of ecosystems management, and her blind hostility to endangered species.

While McCain will take America in the wrong direction—and his policies are nothing but a continuation of eight years of failure—he is real. He is a genuine war hero and has served in the Senate for thirty-five years. Palin, on the other hand, is an avatar, a figment of the right-wing imagination. The fact that nearly half the American people take her seriously is a warning sign that our democracy is in jeopardy. A democracy depends on a population capable of making rational decisions based on facts. Palin is proof we are losing that ability. Karl Rove created her, just as he did George W. Bush, and we know the outcome of that experiment. In the case of Senator John Kerry, Mr. Rove made a war hero into a deserter and an AWOL National Guardsman into a war hero. Rove is up to the same tricks here, molding Palin and her image into a fairy tale completely dissociated from reality.

Barry Goldwater was wrong. Extremism in the defense of freedom is indeed a vice and moderation in the pursuit of justice is in fact a virtue. Extremism undermines the very values purportedly being pursued. But apparently the lessons of the past forty-five years have been lost on Governor Sarah Palin. The Republican candidate for vice president is a religious zealot. In her world, the idea that church must be kept separate from state is merely a quaint relic of liberalism. Palin's extreme religious views do not reflect mainstream American thought and undermine a fundamental tenet of our Constitution.

The governor made the following statement about our troops in Iraq at the Pentecostal Wasilla Assembly of God Church: "Our national leaders are sending them out on a task that is from God; that's what we have to make sure that we're praying for, that there is a plan and that plan is God's plan." This lays bare the idea that the war is a Christian crusade. God supports her war against Islam. If that conclusion is still in doubt, consider that Palin's long-time religious leader, Pastor Kalnins, has openly preached that our invasion of Iraq is a war over the Christian faith. Conveniently, he happens to know that Jesus himself has called upon believers to sacrifice their lives for the war effort. He claims to speak directly to God. I wonder if he would give us stock tips?

When running for governor of Alaska, Palin openly called for teaching creation science in school, alongside evolution. Yes, many Americans would agree, but that is simply a consequence of an educational system in terminal decline. Our students come in sixteenth out of thirty compared to children from around the world. That is why many Americans also believe the earth is four thousand years old rather than 4.5 billion. In a debate during the 2006 gubernatorial election, Palin stated that religious leaders should be able to support a particular candidate from the pulpit, ignoring IRS statutes that prohibit political campaigning by any tax-exempt religious group. That is not terribly surprising coming from her. Her religious mentor, Pastor Kalnins, told followers they would go to hell if they supported Senator Kerry during the 2004 presidential election.

McCain and Palin do not have the character, aptitude, and sense of the American people necessary to tackle our most urgent problems. Their records show quite the opposite. Nothing but a mean streak can explain Palin's documented indifference to rape victims. Nothing but a deeply flawed character can explain her lies about earmarking, suspicious per diem reimbursement claims, or inappropriate meddling in personnel affairs to extract vengeance in a bitter family feud. Nothing but religious zealotry can explain her antiquated views on evolution and her dangerous position on separating church and state. The McCain-Palin team is out of touch with mainstream America.

In sharp contrast, Senators Barak Obama and Joe Biden have articulated a clear plan to address our most urgent problems using methods consistent with the rule of law, our Constitution, and our cherished commitment to core American values. Senator Obama provides us with the personality and policy strength to lead us toward a better future. Obama has the strength of character, wisdom, knowledge, experience, temperament, and steady hand that America needs in these perilous times. By negative example, the horror of the last eight years proves beyond measure that such personality traits are essential to a successful presidency. On every issue, across all elements of society, Senator Obama will return rationality, sanity, and common sense to our government. He will do so to provide security at home and abroad, conserve our natural resources, help families struggling with health care, protect our civil liberties, eliminate America's dependence on foreign oil, and revitalize a government decimated by eight years of malignant neglect.

Let's look at the most critical issues in which President Obama would make the biggest difference in our lives, the lives of our children, and the world we inhabit.

National Security

> Osama bin Laden
> War in Iraq
> Taliban in Afghanistan
> America's standing in the world
> State-sanctioned torture
> Guantanamo Bay
> Domestic terrorism
> Loose nukes
> Port inspections
> Food inspections

Environmental Issues

> Climate change
> Green technologies and the future of U.S. economic
>   strength
> Tropical forests

Coral reefs
Fish stocks
Mining
Endangered species
National forests
Air pollution
Water pollution
Environmental impact studies
Whaling bans
Ecosystems management (wetlands, coastal areas,
    forests)
Plastics and the environment
Recycling
Ice-free poles

Energy Policy

Offshore oil drilling
Renewable energy
Nuclear energy

Social Policy

Sex education
Stem cell research
Abortion
Supreme Court nominees
Foreign assistance
Family values

Economic Policy

Federal debt and deficit
Collapsing financial markets

Tax breaks
Foreclosures epidemic

Good Government

Voting systems that Americans can trust
Rational national health care system
Widespread and numerous scandals
Federal scientific advisory system
Earmarks and pork-barrel spending
Sanctity of life
Separation of church and state
Creation science and intelligent design
National disaster responses
Sex scandals
Cronyism and corruption
First Amendment rights
Second Amendment rights
Bridge to nowhere but lies
Government chefs
Minimum qualification standards

The dual issues of national security and climate change are the yin and yang of global challenges most urgently in need of rational policy. The two are closely linked. While terrorism and radical Islam are the most immediate threats, degradation of the environment—and depletion of the resources on which we depend—presents an even greater, although longer-term challenge to our national security.

Osama bin Laden

Let's be crystal clear about one point that President Bush consistently lies about: Al Qaeda was not in Iraq prior to our invasion; Al Qaeda was not influencing Saddam Hussein, and Iraq had nothing, absolutely nothing, to do with the attacks of 9/11. That is the unambiguous conclusion from every National Intelligence Estimate (NIE) and of the Iraq Study Group. But President Bush continues to lie. In his deception of the American people, Bush cannot, however, obscure the saddest fact: the one man most responsible for 9/11 is still at large, Osama bin Laden, is making videos like a Spielberg protégé. Worse, as a direct consequence of our invasion, Al Qaeda has "reconstituted its core structure along the Pakistani border and may now be a stronger and more resilient organization today than it appeared a year ago," according to the most recent NIE. John McCain is not a maverick on these issues. He agrees with the discredited and consistently wrong President Bush.

Worse still, as we divert a trillion dollars to a hopeless war, we ignore our most urgent national security threats. Today nearly 90 percent of all cargo entering the United States remains uninspected. Our food supply is completely vulnerable. Our water is unprotected, as are our nuclear power plants. We remain unprepared for biological or chemical attacks. All these years later, many local, state, and national emergency response teams still don't have a coordinated means of communicating.

We've diverted all our resources from our most urgent needs. The one indisputable result of our invasion of Iraq is that we are now more vulnerable than we have ever been. Bush's monomaniacal and blind effort to "stay the course" and McCain's support for it is now our greatest threat to national security.

In September 2006, in a statement dripping with unintended irony, Bush accused the Democrats of cherry-picking pieces of the then recently declassified NIE report "for partisan political gain . . . to mislead the American people and justify their policy of withdrawal from Iraq." Cherry-picking? How about cherry-picking faulty intelligence, ignoring glaring inconsistencies, and persecuting those in disagreement as the Cheney Gang marched us off to war? While the majority of Americans now realize we were duped into this war by a dishonest administration, few ask why or how this came about. The answer lies in the Bush administration's faith-based approach to reality. When you have a hotline to heaven, you must be right. The Bush administration has declared a war on reason, demonstrating a consistent antipathy to science and logic. One result is the Iraq war.

Iraq is a religious war because Bush believes he is carrying out God's mandate in executing the war. He has reportedly said that "I believe God wants me to be president." If accurate—and multiple sources over time have reported similar quotes—those are perhaps the most frightening words ever spoken in American history. In response to 9/11, Bush claimed a mandate "to answer these attacks and rid the world of evil . . . We will export death and violence to the four corners of the earth in defense of this great nation." That of course leaves him free to define evil, all while exporting death. But with a divine mandate, that is justifiable. We need to reclaim logic in our foreign policy and move away from faith-based policy making. The world will be a safer place. And let's catch bin Laden.

Iraq War

Perhaps nothing better defines the difference between McCain and Obama than their respective positions on the war in Iraq. Obama was right and McCain was wrong. The war in Iraq is indisputably the worst foreign policy disaster this country has ever faced. Obama opposed the war from the start. McCain supported Bush when he initiated this conflict under the false pretense of ever-shifting rationales based on fabricated evidence and then executed the war with criminal incompetence.

Every proclamation from Bush, Cheney, Rumsfeld, and the cabal of neocons at the Pentagon has been proven wrong, staring with weapons of mass destruction and falsely linking Iraq to the attacks of September 11. In May 2003, standing under the now infamous "Mission Accomplished" sign Bush said, "Major combat operations in Iraq have ended. In the battle of Iraq, the United States and our allies have prevailed." Just a few months earlier, in March 2003, Cheney said, "My belief is we will, in fact, be greeted as liberators." In June 2005, in discussing the insurgency, Cheney predicted, "I think they're in the last throes, if you will, of the insurgency."

So now Bush and McCain both claim that the February 2007 Iraq War "surge" of an additional 30,000 troops has worked, and that Obama was wrong to oppose an increase in troops. Since every other proclamation from Bush has been spectacularly wrong, the problem of credibility arises. But let's take the claim at face value and assume that large numbers of American troops resulted in a decrease in violence. How does that constitute this grand "victory" proclaimed by Bush and McCain? The original idea was to create space and time to enable the establishment of a political solution to reduce civil strife. That has not happened, and now McCain talks of long-term engagements in Iraq. Proof that the surge was unsuccessful is evident in Bush's troop withdrawal announcement, which pulls out only eight thousand of the additional thirty thousand soldiers. If the surge was successful, by definition all the soldiers included in the surge could come home. That is what *surge* means: a big push in followed by withdrawal. Otherwise we simply have deployment of more troops, in spite of the desperate convolution of the language to describe the action.

But even if the surge had worked exactly as advertised, Obama was right all along. Claiming success for the surge makes sense only in the context of a just war, but every aspect of the war has been thoroughly discredited. Neither Bush nor McCain has ever been able to define success in Iraq for the simple reason that success is not possible in the absence of a clear mission. Weapons of mass destruction? Saving Iraqis from Saddam's wrath? Promoting democracy? Securing oil supplies? Punishing Iraq for Saudi hijackers protected by the Taliban in Afghanistan? No blunder in the history of this great nation can match the tragic miscalculations in Iraq. On the war in Iraq, Obama was right, Bush and McCain were wrong, and no amount of hand waving can make that fact go away.

Guantanamo Bay

Even the most blindly patriotic American should hide in shame in the face of the kangaroo court conviction of bin Laden's former driver. Salim Hamdan may well be guilty and deserving of a life in prison. But we will never know, because the trial at Guantanamo Bay was a farce, an embarrassment to all Americans. Secret evidence, closed proceedings, testimony tainted by coercion, hearsay evidence, the inability to confront one's accusers, and a stacked jury made a mockery of justice. The jury of Hamdan's peers consisted of six senior military officers. One can imagine their career opportunities should they have decided to exonerate the defendant. Military courts do not adhere to anything close to what the average American expects from the rule of law. We condone torture and convict suspects in sham trials. We have lost our moral bearing. To save our way of life we are destroying its foundation.

Domestic Terrorism: Anthrax and Other Forgotten Threats

Sixteen bombs killed three and badly injured sixteen. A bomb killed 168 people and maimed another eight hundred. Anthrax killed five people, sickened seventeen, shut down the capital, and frightened a nation. Beirut? Baghdad? No, the terrorists were not Al Qaeda operatives or Muslim extremists hiding in an Afghan cave, but all-American boys killing right here at home. Our home-grown killers were mathematician Ted Kaczynski, baby-faced Tim McVeigh, and, allegedly, army researcher Bruce E. Ivins. Ivins' suicide and the FBI's bungled investigation remind us that we fiddle while Rome burns.

We have created a haven and breeding ground for a new generation of terrorists in Iraq. Our ports remain unprotected; only 10 percent of containers entering the country are inspected. Our food is uninspected. Salmonella outbreaks alone sicken 1.4 million Americans each year and kill one thousand people. This bug will kill as many people in three years as died on 9/11. Our water supplies are unprotected. Our nuclear facilities are unguarded. For eight years we have diverted resources away from the gravest threats to our security. We need to redefine our security needs and then redeploy our assets to best protect us from internal and external dangers.

Climate Change

No other single environmental challenge has the potential to alter our lives more profoundly than the accelerated warming of our planet. The scientific community harbors absolutely no doubt about the reality of climate change; any doubts still lingering are the result of a well-funded disinformation campaign by the petroleum, utility, and mining industries. The vast preponderance of scientific opinion, from virtually every country on the globe, accepts that climate change is real. More than twenty-five hundred scientists from 166 countries have concluded unambiguously that climate change is real and caused by human activity. Barak Obama understands the urgency of this issue and will commit to reducing our greenhouse gas emissions by 50 percent by the year 2050. He has vowed to make the United States a leader once again in combating global warming. But "*the jury is still out*," according to Palin, who is smarter than those twenty-five hundred climate experts. Based on her expertise in climatology, she dismisses climate change as a left-wing conspiracy, in opposition to her running mate. She denies that the dramatic melting of arctic ice has anything to do with global warming caused by human activity.

Obama is right. McCain and Palin are wrong. The year 2006 was the warmest ever recorded since the Federal Government began formally keeping historic weather records in 1895. The first two hurricanes in 2007 were Category 5 storms, the first time that has happened since

1851, the first year on record. There have been thirty-one Category 5 hurricanes since 1851; eight of them occurred in the past four years. We already have Gustav, Hanna, Ike, and Jeannine in 2008, with more storms in tow. We are playing with fire because we don't know all the consequences of the changes we are creating. Just one small example: more warming in the west allowed the cold-sensitive bark beetle to proliferate, ravaging once-cool western forests.

Of the world's 300 million people who live less than fifteen feet above sea level, 80 percent are in developing countries: 200 million in Asia (90 million in China alone); 17 million in the Middle East and North Africa; 11 million in sub-Saharan Africa, and 8 million in Latin America and the Caribbean. Rapid sea-level rise will threaten millions with flooding; there will also be more severe flooding from storm surges and abnormally high tides.

A total melting of the current Greenland ice sheet would result in a sea-level rise of about twenty feet; melting of the west Antarctic ice sheet would result in a sea-level rise of about twenty feet. The west Antarctic ice sheet is especially vulnerable because much of it is grounded below sea level. If both the west Antarctic and Greenland ice sheets melted, we would see a sea-level rise of thirty feet, which would flood about 25 percent of the U.S. population.

The United States has 5 percent of the world's population but contributes 25 percent of all greenhouse gas emissions. Yet we still bury our heads in the sand, cite "uncertainty," and do nothing to prevent global warming. The United States should be leading the world but instead has become a silent spectator. Our reward will be more Katrinas, more flooding, trillions of dollars in damages, and a true threat to our national security and economy.

In spite of the McCain-Palin effort to paint global warming as a liberal plot, a group of twenty-eight institutional investors, managing more than a trillion dollars in assets, called on the Securities and Exchange Commission (SEC) to change the rules on public disclosure to include the impact of climate change on the bottom line. The group wants the SEC to require all publicly traded companies to disclose the financial risks of climate change in routine financial reporting to the public. They base this request on the SEC's rule that companies must disclose any "known trends, events or uncertainties that are reasonably likely to have a material effect on a company's financial condition."

Brushing off the notion that climate change is not real, these folks controlling one trillion dollars want the industries most impacted by climate change to fess up and admit to the pending financial burden. This includes the insurance industry, which will have to pay claims on damage caused by an increase in the intensity and number of storms, coastal erosion, and sea-level rise. On the other end of the spectrum are industries that might be impacted by greenhouse gas emission limitations, such as those in the energy sector and auto companies. This group of money managers is not a cabal of liberal left-wingers wearing Al Gore T-shirts singing "Kumbaya." Instead, these scions of American monetary might need to act on the fact of a complete void of leadership in Washington, which continues to deny the obvious. McCain, and Bush before him, have fully abdicated the domestic and global responsibility to tackle the issue of climate change, forcing individual states and industry to take matters into their own hands. Actions by individual states and industry giants are important, but ultimately are no substitute for federal leadership. Any effective actions to address climate change must be based on global cooperation, which can only be realized through concerted government action at the highest levels. Such action, sadly, must wait until we have a new president who gets it. McCain is not that man; Obama is. Iraq may define Bush's presidency now, but history will judge him more harshly for six years of malignant neglect, wasting critical years in humanity's epic battle to preserve the resources that sustain us.

Along with the impact on financial markets, also often overlooked with climate change are the potentially catastrophic impacts on public health. We will see an expanding range of tropical diseases, new strains of old diseases as they move north, more and more severe allergies as ragweed season grows longer, more mold and fungus in hotter more humid weather, change in rainfall patterns affecting food production, more extreme heat waves, and more frequent and severe droughts and longer and more intense fire season. As warmer weather moves north, disease vectors go along for the ride. Many of those vectors are insects, like mosquitoes, which are expanding their range to a backyard near you. Water-borne diseases will increase in frequency because warmer water expands the season and range of diseases-causing organisms. Rodents also proliferate in the growing temperate regions with milder wet winters; they themselves are disease carriers, and also are reservoirs for disease-carrying ticks.

The result is not pretty. In addition to more summertime barbecues, we can look forward to a host of ugly diseases, including dengue fever, malaria, yellow fever, hantavirus, leptospirosis, Japanese B encephalitis, elephantiasis, Lyme disease, West Nile virus, leishmaniasis, Chagas' disease, and typhus. At the same time, climate change is wreaking havoc with bird reproduction, resulting in a decline of 75 percent of all bird species. Those birds were eating insects. With fewer birds to eat the bugs, not only will the pests be moving into the United States, where they've never been before, but there will be more of them than ever, across the expanded range. In Sweden, we are already seeing disease-bearing ticks moving north as winters become warmer. Not a good sign for the United States and those who would rather not contract Lyme disease.

Severe drought in the Southwest has reduced predator populations, leading to an explosion of white-footed mice, which carry Hantavirus. New Yorkers first suffered an outbreak of West Nile virus in 1999, a new scourge for the city, which is now an annual threat. We will also get new strains of old diseases. A new strain of West Nile, first detected in 2002, is moving quickly. The virus infected about 175,000 people in 2007, killing 117. But flying and crawling critters bringing the gift of new disease are not the only problem. You will be sneezing more as well. An increase in carbon dioxide supercharges the growth of the most aggressive pollen producers, including hay-fever-causing ragweed and the trees that give us the worst springtime allergies. But we're not done. While we fight off noxious mosquitoes and dab our running noses, we will also be swatting more wasps and yellow jackets. These stinging beasts are already showing up in parts of Alaska where they've never been seen before.

You might retreat to your basement to get away from it all, but you'll find no safe haven there. With a warmer climate we will see an increase in the proliferation of mold and fungus, the spores of which love warmer temperatures and higher levels of carbon dioxide. Severe droughts in Africa lead to massive dust storms from that continent's expanding deserts. Those clouds travel across the Atlantic and into the lungs of unsuspecting citizens in Florida, who have seen a twentyfold rise in asthma in the past several decades. At a broader level, changing weather patterns will bring floods to some areas and more severe droughts to others, a longer and more extreme fire season, and changes to agricultural production, all of which are direct threats to human health. For some, the threat of sea-level rise, loss of arctic ice, or the impacts of more frequent and extreme storms are not enough to take climate change seriously.

Perhaps the possibility of contracting a nasty tropical disease will finally be a wake-up call. But not for McCain-Palin. No, the Bush administration is actively blocking any actions to address the issue of climate change, and a McCain-Palin administration would do the same. In January 2008, Bush prevented California and other states from adopting tighter restrictions on greenhouse gas emissions from vehicles. Of course, Bush walked away from the Kyoto Protocol, in which the world agreed to limit emission of greenhouse gases—another position McCain agreed with.

Green Technologies The biggest transformation our children will experience in their lives compared to ours is the shift from fossil fuels to renewable energies. The country that masters these and other green technologies will be the next century's economic superpower. Obama's plan to promote renewable energy sources such as wind and solar power will alone create 5 million new high-paying jobs. But that is just the tip of the iceberg, assuming any icebergs remain in our warming world.

China is putting on line a new coal-fired power plant every day. Chinese coal is dirty, chockfull of sulphur. Developing countries in Asia and Africa reasonably focus more on short-term growth than long-term environmental issues. These countries will not listen to a browbeating by the United States. We must lead by example. The first country to master green technology and renewable energy will be the next economic superpower.

We sit at the threshold of the next industrial revolution. The mantle of global leader is ours to lose, and it appears that is what we may well do unless we recognize the imperative of green technology. We need leadership at the national level to shift from fossil fuels to renewables;

to evolve rapidly to a hydrogen economy; to turn trash to cash; to instill efficiency at all levels of production and minimize materials consumption and waste in homes, farms, and factories; to encourage green construction in houses and offices; to leapfrog to the next generation of battery and energy storage technology; and to develop the technologies that will be needed to mitigate the impacts of climate change.

Just as the United States became globally dominant through technology and innovation in the 1800s and 1900s, the next two centuries will belong to the country that first embraces and encourages the technologies that promote both green and growth. But that will not happen under McCain-Palin. "Drill here and drill now" and "Drill, baby, drill" are not the cries of a team interested in supporting a transition to renewable energy and green technology.

Stem Cell Research

Spouting pious platitudes about the sanctity of life, right-wing Republicans led by Bush have prevented federal funding of stem cell research. In a morally contemptible twist of logic, Bush allowed research to go forward on a few cell lines proven to be of limited use. Stem cell research holds promise for curing terrible diseases like Alzheimer's, Parkinson's, spinal cord injury, rheumatoid arthritis, and cancer. President Bush and now McCain-Palin value a microscopic dot of cells smaller than the period at the end of this sentence over the life of a wounded soldier in a wheelchair. As a result of the Bush moratorium, expertise in this critical area of research is being lost overseas. The United States is in danger of becoming a second-class research base behind Australia, Singapore, Israel, Sweden, and Finland. Those are the countries poised to find cures for the most debilitating diseases of our times. We need a president who will actively support stem cell research and reinvigorate America's commitment to cutting-edge science. We need to elect Barak Obama.

Tropical Forests

We are destroying tropical forests, and all the biological diversity they contain, at an ever-increasing rate of almost 40 million acres every year. Bush does not care much. Neither do Mc-Cain-Palin. In 2003, the most current year with accurate statistics, saw a record ten thousand square miles of forests cleared in Brazil alone. The World Resources Institute predicts that at present rates of deforestation, up to 35 percent of all closed canopy forest species will be lost. Humankind is witnessing the loss of nearly 140 species every day. Rain forests once covered 14 percent of the earth's surface, but now cover only 6 percent. At current rates of destruction, the dwindling forests that remain will be consumed completely in forty years. Loss of tropical forests is expected to result in the extinction of half of the world's species. That would include many of direct benefit to humankind in the form of food, medicine, and materials. Just 2.5 acres of tropical forest contain 750 types of trees and fifteen hundred species of plants. More than three thousand edible fruits are found in the rain forests, only two hundred of which are currently used in Western countries. In spite of the compelling need for action McCain-Palin are indifferent to the economic, social, and environmental costs of tropical deforestation.

Biological Diversity The rate of extinction is now a thousand times the natural rate. Up to 30 percent of all mammals, birds, and reptiles are threatened with extinction. We have already lost more than 10 percent of all plant species. Yet policies influenced by religion result in the United States walking away from the Rio treaty to protect biological diversity. As far back as June 1994, the Senate Foreign Relations Committee approved ratification of the Convention on Biological Diversity by a lopsided vote of sixteen to three. That would be the last victory. Bush's persistent opposition to saving rapidly declining diversity killed any hope that the United States would sign the treaty. While seemingly a platitude, extinction is indeed forever. The world cannot endure a McCain-Palin repeat of the Bush administration before taking action to conserve biological diversity. Too much is at stake; we need to elect Obama.

Coral Reefs More than one-quarter of the world's coral reefs are dead or severely damaged, while an additional one-third are seriously degraded or threatened. Why care? Reefs are home to the larvae of, or an important source of food for, almost every important commercial fishery. Coral reefs provide about $375 billion worth of economic and environmental services each year. About 500 million people live within just sixty miles of a coral reef, and benefit directly from the reefs' productivity and protection they provide from the ocean's wrath. The Great Barrier Reef alone supports about 8 percent of all of the world's fish species. Reefs are extremely sensitive to any change in seawater temperatures. We now estimate that 70 percent of all reefs will disappear in the next fifty years, largely due to global warming. Yet another reason why we need to elect a president to "gets it." That would be Obama.

Fish Stocks

The ocean provides us with food, raw materials, a medium for transportation, recreation, and a source of life-saving drugs. But what was once considered a source of unlimited abundance now needs to be carefully managed. This frightening indicator of global environmental degradation is largely overlooked by the public and media. Humans have depleted 90 percent of all large fish from the world's oceans. That includes pelagic fish like tuna, swordfish, and marlin, as well as bottom and coastal fish like cod, halibut, and flounder. Since 1950, we have nearly wiped out every large fish in every ocean, pole to pole.

About 60 percent of the world's population lives in coastal areas. Human population growth in coastal zones is about twice that of the global population growth. Worldwide, about one billion people rely on fish as their main source of protein. But overfishing, coastal erosion from badly managed developments, pollution, and loss of critical habitats are threatening the resource. The problem extends beyond the obvious loss of a major source of nutrition for the world's hungry. With dramatic losses of megafauna and primary predators, we will likely see major dislocations and significant changes in marine ecosystems that could impact the entire food chain.

We cannot rely upon the usual magic of market forces so dear to Bush, McCain, Palin, and friends to moderate demand as supplies dwindle and prices rise to reflect that scarcity. Instead, consumers are willing to pay more and more, to the point where fishing a species to extinction becomes economical. A medium-sized tuna can now sell for over $200,000. That provides great incentive to get out the old nets and fire up the diesel. In addition, our government has provided perverse incentives that promote overexploitation. Government subsidies vainly attempt to shore up dwindling jobs and preserve a way of life, but only delay the inevitable. Those jobs and communities will be lost when no more fish can be caught. All the government has done under Republican leadership is to ensure the final destruction of the fish stock.

Endangered Species Act

Palin is a danger to endangered species. She argued strenuously against listing the polar bear, stating that the decision was based on "unproven long-term impact of any future climate change on the species." Palin was concerned that listing the polar bear would "*do serious long-term damage to the vibrant economy of the Cook Inlet area.*" (Speaking of Cook Inlet, Palin also opposes any listing of the beluga whales found there, even though the whale's numbers have declined dramatically over the past twenty years.) All biologists know that shrinking polar ice threatens the survival of polar bears, yet Palin dismisses the entire problem—both the shrinking ice itself and the cause of that shrinking. Less than one month before being chosen as John McCain's running mate, Palin actively supported the Bush administration's eight-year war on the Endangered Species Act. With Palin's approval, Alaska sued the federal government on August 4, 2008, for listing the polar bear as a threatened species. The lawsuit claimed that taking such action would be detrimental to "oil and gas . . . development" in Alaska. But that assault was not sufficiently aggressive for Palin, who claimed that listing the polar bear as endangered should be rescinded because such a listing "was not based on the best scientific and commercial data available."

This is the woman who dismisses the conclusion of twenty-five hundred climate scientists. So Palin is not only an expert climatologist, but an ecologist too. As a result, McCain-Palin will continue the persistent effort by George W. Bush to prevent putting new animals and plants on the endangered species list. The statistics are startling. In the past eight years, only fifty-nine species have made the list under Bush, compared to fifty-eight every year under George W.'s father, and sixty-two per year under Clinton. This obstinacy has real and tragic consequences.

A sockeye salmon and pygmy rabbit, for example, went extinct after Bush prevented their listing. McCain-Palin are an environmental disaster area, and we need to prevent them from occupying the White House.

National Forests

In a blatant frontal assault on the environment, the Bush administration pushed to open up 35 percent of our national forests to roads, logging, and mining. The area at stake encompasses nearly 60 million acres of pristine woodlands. Bush pushed for more intense and more widespread logging in national forests. He did so even though every major study shows that such logging makes no economic sense. Forest protection actually creates more jobs, generates more income, and results in greater tax revenues than logging. Ecological functions like water filtration, erosion and flood protection, carbon sequestration, and habitat protection for agricultural pollinators combine with tourism to provide a sustainable revenue source that vastly exceeds income from logging.

Air Pollution

Republicans seem to be offended by clean air and clear vistas in our national parks. So much so that the Bush administration has proposed a rule change that threatens air quality by modifying how air pollution is measured in our nation's iconic wilderness areas. Existing rules logically seek to ensure that national parks provide visitors with the cleanest air by imposing the strictest safeguards against pollution. But the change would allow coal-fired power plants to be built adjacent to parks, ignoring the impact of smog and haze. Apparently Republicans pine for an urban experience when visiting woodlands.

That assault on reason and air quality is not enough, however. The rules would also allow seventeen thousand existing power plants to dump pollutants into the air with abandon. While the relaxed pollution standard is being proposed by the Environmental Protection Agency (EPA), many of that organization's own scientists oppose the change. Such opposition is understandable because this action would undermine a key component of the Clean Air Act, recognized globally as one of the most successful pieces of environmental legislation ever enacted.

Making a mockery of law, Republicans want to subvert the restrictions imposed in 1977. Under the original legislation, existing plants at the time of enactment were exempted until the time the plant did any major upgrade. Routine maintenance was excluded. But the Bush administration redefined "routine maintenance" in a way that essentially guts the law, allowing a plant to virtually rebuild without meeting modern pollution standards. The result will be thirty-four tons of mercury dumped into the air in 2010, an amount six times what would have been emitted under enforcement of the Clean Air Act. The Bush-McCain-Palin approach to mercury is particularly sad because the economically viable technologies exist to reduce mercury pollution by 90 percent. The Republicans won't be satisfied until we have dense smog that offers all of us air we can taste.

Water Pollution Bush encourages regulators to ignore enforcement of the Clean Water Act, threatening the quality of 20 million acres of wetlands and tens of thousands of miles of streams, rivers, and lakes. The Republicans have single-handedly halted and reversed thirty years of progress. In a sick twist on law enforcement, the Bush administration directed all EPA and U.S. Army Corps of Engineers field staff to stop taking any actions to protect any water until first obtaining permission from national headquarters, which really meant, ultimately, the White House. Staff needed permission to enforce the law!

Bush actually tried to reduce tougher federal standards for arsenic and mercury in drinking water. This, in spite of the undisputed fact that mercury has contaminated 130 million acres of lakes and 800,000 miles of streams and rivers. That matters because mercury causes developmental and neurological problems at extremely low concentrations. When Democrats overturned Bush's relaxed standards, Senate Republicans, including John McCain, stepped up to the plate to reintroduce legislation to reduce water quality standards in rural areas.

Mining Mayhem

McCain's choice of running mate opposed restrictions on mining operations in Alaska that could impact salmon in streams and rivers. She is accused of abusing her power as governor by improperly weighing in on a ballot initiative to oppose the clean water initiative. A legal complaint has been filed against her. She specifically opposed any efforts to stop the Pebble Mine, which if approved would be the largest open-pit gold and copper mine in North America. Palin is unconcerned that the mine would pollute Bristol Bay's headwaters. She actively opposed efforts that were aimed specifically at preventing the mine from dumping waste materials directly into salmon watersheds.

Offshore Oil Drilling in ANWR

Palin subscribes to the notion that God put resources here on earth for man's exploitation, as described in Genesis. She believes God is not only on her side, but supports her specific environmental and energy policies. Concerning a proposed $30 billion gas pipeline in Alaska, she actually said, "I think God's will has to be done in unifying people and companies to get that gas line built, so pray for that." God takes time out from Darfur, terrorism, disease, hunger, and suffering to make sure Palin gets her pipeline. Her answer to our energy needs, with God's approval: Drill, baby, drill. Her version of energy independence is to drill for more oil. She wants to *"drill here, drill now."*

Palin opposed her own running mate, prior to becoming his vice-presidential choice, and wants to drill in the Arctic National Wildlife Refuge (ANWR), one of the world's last pristine ecosystems. The most optimistic estimates put peak production at 780,000 barrels per day from ANWR; the United States consumes 21 million barrels per day. So even at maximum output, ANWR would supply less than 4 percent of our daily consumption. And that peak would quickly fall to under 700,000 barrels per day. For that she wants to destroy millions of unspoiled acres. Drilling in ANWR solves no problems. Oil production produces a budget surplus in a state with less than 700,000 residents. But Palin did not invest those funds into renewable energy sources to wean us from oil; no, she proposed distributing the money to each individual in the state. We can no more drill our way out of this mess than an alcoholic can drink his way to sobriety. The idea is pure nonsense, and delays critical actions necessary to secure our future.

Renewable Energy

Typical of Republican subterfuge, McCain says one thing but does another, consistently opposing renewable energy while claiming to be a supporter. The Bush energy policy announced in 2001 was based on closed-door recommendations from coal, oil, and nuclear energy companies. While giving a weak nod to renewables, Bush cut millions of dollars from existingrenewable energy programs just five weeks later. In March 2008, Bush opposed passage of the Renewable Energy and Energy Conservation Tax Act (H.R. 5351), which would have extended tax credits to promote renewables. Energy producers and homeowners would benefit when installing or using wind, solar, or geothermal energy sources.

Obama supports exactly the right approach to a sustainable energy future, setting realistic goals using reasonable incentives. He will invest $150 billion over the next ten years to catalyze private efforts to build a clean energy future. Under this plan, within ten years the United States will save more oil than we currently import from the Middle East and Venezuela combined. Obama will put one million plug-in hybrid cars on the road by 2015. These cars can achieve up to 150 miles per gallon and will be built in America. Obama will ensure that at least 10 percent of our electricity comes from renewable sources by 2012 and 25 percent by 2025. This program will keep the United States at the forefront of emerging green technologies so critical to the health of our economy. In stark contrast, McCain gives tax breaks to oil companies earning record profits and pushes nuclear energy. This perpetuates a losing strategy and endangers America's ability to compete in the green economies of the future.

Nuclear Energy

John McCain plans to build forty-five new nuclear power plants by 2030 as a means of reducing greenhouse gas emissions. Amazingly, this plan is taken directly from Bush's failed National Energy Policy, the brainchild of Dick Cheney and his secret advisers seven long years ago. Like Bush, McCain wants an expanded nuclear energy industry to be a "major component" in the nation's energy policy. We have "McBush" once again, the twins being so close on so many issues that the two cannot be seen as separate individuals. Sadly, Senator McCain fails to address the primary problem with nuclear energy: waste disposal. He has no plan. The Yucca Mountain Repository in Nevada was scheduled to begin accepting nuclear waste in 1998. The earliest date now mentioned to start construction is 2013, with a completion date of 2017. But those dates are no more likely than 1998. Until this issue is addressed, reliance on nuclear energy is either a pipe dream or a radioactive nightmare, but certainly not a solution to our energy problems.

International Whaling

The International Whaling Commission (IWC) is under intense pressure from Japan, Iceland, and Norway to lift the ban on commercial whaling, in place since 1986. Here is an environmental issue that requires strong leadership from the United States. The rationale put forward by the three nations is not supported by facts. Whales do not deplete fish stocks, because 99 percent of the time they feed in areas of little or no commercial fishing. Whale oil is no longer needed. No market exists for whale meat. In Japan, the government forces the commodity on unwilling participants. An example is forcing school cafeterias to serve whale meat. The product sits wasted on store shelves. Given the weak political structure of the IWC, only coherent, consistent, and forceful leadership can prevent this ban from being lifted. We need a president who cares. We need Obama.

Ecosystems Management Palin the environmental scientist and ecologist has promoted initiatives to let citizens shoot wolves from airplanes and helicopters; she promotes weakening bear hunting laws in order to reduce bear populations. Why? So there will be more moose and caribou to draw big-game hunters to the state. We need not say more.

The North Pole Canada, Russia, Denmark and Norway are now jockeying for control of new shipping routes and mining opportunities opened up in the Arctic as a consequence of global warming, all while Bush and his conservative allies sit on the sidelines denying the reality of climate change.

Canada recently sent warships to the Arctic to claim sovereignty. Russia for the first time since the end of the Cold War sent twelve of its strategic bombers flying to the Arctic; but if that did not make the point, a Russian submarine planted that nation's flag on the ocean floor directly under the North Pole. Why the sudden spate of territorial claims? The European Space Agency reported on September 15 that satellites now confirm that Arctic ice has shrunk to the lowest level on record. Polar ice now covers 25 percent less area than just three decades ago, and is one-third thinner. Melting ice opens up a sea lane and exposes a vast territory to exploitation of immense mineral wealth.

Since the late fifteenth century, mariners have searched for the so-called Northwest Passage, a viable route to join the Atlantic and Pacific Oceans through the Arctic Archipelago. Since the first effort in 1576, all the expeditions ended in failure, disaster, and tragedy. The waters and ice were simply too treacherous. But in spite of deadly obstacles, the search held tremendous allure because a sea route between Europe and Asia through the Arctic would be about forty-five hundred miles shorter than the route through the Panama Canal. President Thomas Jefferson, never one to give up easily, decided to send Lewis and Clark in 1804 across the unexplored reaches of the continent to determine if rivers might offer an alternate water route west. That, too, proved to be impossible, although their expedition was a success for other reasons. The Northwest Passage through the Arctic was actually made in 1903 and 1906 by the famous Norwegian explorer Roald Amundsen, but the course was never viable as a commercial route due to the hostile nature of the north seas.

All of that is now changing, and fast, thanks to global warming. The ice seems immune to Republican denials and continues to melt at unprecedented rates. An ice-free Northwest Passage during the summer might be good for shipping, but bad for the world in general. Snow reflects sunlight, but water absorbs the sun's heat. With less ice, more heat is absorbed, leading to more melting, leading to more heat absorption, leading to more melting. That feedback loop accelerates global warming. The likely consequence is a catastrophic rise in sea level, which would dwarf the devastation we saw in New Orleans from Katrina.

McCain will not take actions to prevent or mitigate a problem he denies exists. So while the rest of the world acts, the United States remains on the sidelines. We have abdicated a leadership role on the world stage at a time when our apathy threatens every aspect of our way of life. We can only hope that Obama is elected; he will reverse the madness of the Bush administration, and work concertedly to address the issue of climate change to protect our sovereignty, security, and environment.

Recycling   Recycling yields eight primary benefits by: (1) reducing the need for new landfills, (2) saving energy, (3) reducing air and water pollution, (4) creating jobs, (5) supplying valuable raw materials to industry, (6) reducing greenhouse gas emissions, (7) helping to conserve natural resources, and (8) stimulating development of green technologies.

• Economic Benefits

Recycling creates 1.1 million U.S. jobs, $236 billion in gross annual sales and $37 billion in annual payrolls. For every job collecting recyclables, there are twenty-six jobs in processing the materials and manufacturing them into new products. Recycling creates four jobs for every one job created in the waste management and disposal industries.

• Environmental Benefits

Recycling and composting diverted nearly 70 million tons of material away from landfills and incinerators in 2000, up from 34 million tons in 1990—doubling in just ten years. Every ton of paper that is recycled equals the output from seventeen trees. In my hometown of Austin, we save about six hundred pine trees every day by recycling newspapers. The energy we save when we recycle one glass bottle is enough to light a lightbulb for four hours.

In the United States, processing minerals contributes almost half of all reported toxic emissions from industry, sending 1.5 million tons of pollution into the air and water each year. Recycling can significantly reduce these emissions. It takes 95 percent less energy to recycle aluminum than it does to make it from raw materials. Manufacturing cans from recycled aluminum produces 96 percent less air and water pollution than manufacturing cans from raw material (bauxite). Making recycled steel saves 60 percent in energy use, recycled newspaper 50 percent, recycled plastics 70 percent, and recycled glass

40 percent. These savings far outweigh the energy created as by-products of incineration. In 2005, recycling conservatively saved the amount of energy used in 9 million homes (900 trillion BTUs).

A national recycling rate of 30 percent reduces greenhouse gas emissions as much as removing nearly 25 million cars from the road. Specifically, for example, just recycling steel cans used in the food industry reduced greenhouse gas emissions by the equivalent of 600,000 metric tons of carbon. But all McCain-Palin want to do is drill, baby, drill. Obama has a rational, comprehensive, strategic plan to protect our environment.

Plastics and the Environment

Climate change rightfully gets the headlines, but another environmental problem looms underneath. Not one artifact salvaged from the *Titanic* was plastic. Yet plastics are now ubiquitous in our lives, found in our computers, cell phones, pens, carpets, flooring, blinds, pipes, credit cards, kitchen gadgets, cars, planes, and clothes. But the advantages and benefits of plastics have made them essential to everyday modern life. Plastics are durable, lightweight, cheap, non-breakable, and versatile. For every seven trucks needed to deliver paper grocery bags to the store, only one truck is needed to carry the same number of plastic grocery bags. Compared to paper grocery bags, plastic bags consume 40 percent less energy; generate 80 percent less solid waste; produce 70 percent fewer emissions and release 94 percent fewer waterborne wastes. Plastics make up about 28 percent by volume of all trash overall, but because it can be compressed, only about 10 percent of landfill volume. In 1999, 14 million trees were cut down to make 10 billion paper grocery bags. A plastic grocery bag costs one cent versus four cents for paper.

Plastic lumber, made with recycled plastic, holds nails and screws better than wood, is virtually maintenance free, and lasts for fifty years. Foam polystyrene containers take 30 percent less total energy to make than paperboard containers. Between 1990 and 1996 the amount of waste going into landfills declined by more than 17 percent by weight. By using plastic in packaging, American product manufacturers save enough energy each year to power a city of one million homes for three and a half years. Today, over twelve thousand communities provide recycling services to 184 million people. The postconsumer plastics recycling industry provides jobs for more than fifty-two thousand American workers.

But not all is good and nice. The United States produced about 245 million tons (49 trillion pounds) in 2006; about 12 percent was some kind of plastic. In the United States, about 12 million barrels of oil are used each year to make plastic bags alone. Plastic bags have become the urban tumbleweed. Between 500 billion and 1 trillion plastic grocery bags are consumed worldwide each year; 84 billion in the United States, 19 billion in California. Less than 3 percent are recycled, while many are reused as trashcan liners, lunch bags, and laundry bags; many wind up as litter.

Half of all marine pollution is plastic. Nearly 90 percent of trash recently observed in the North Pacific was plastic. Plastic bags are estimated to kill one million sea creatures each year, including whales, seals, and turtles; plastic bags act as rafts to allow nonnative species to spread around the world. Sea turtles mistake plastic bags for jellyfish.

Plastic pellets, the raw form plastic is often transported in to manufacturing facilities, are now ubiquitous in the marine environment; an EPA study found pellets in thirteen out of fourteen harbors tested. Thirty-five of the forty-seven most carcinogenic chemicals used in manufacturing are involved in plastics production. PVC (polyvinyl chloride) is considered the worst, creating more hazardous byproducts in its lifecycle than any other product. Dioxin is released when chlorine is combined with ethylene to make PVC. *Bisphenol-A*, used to make plastic firm, and *phthalates*, used to make plastics pliable, mimic human sex hormones; these chemicals leach from containers into our food supply.

In 2003, 40 million plastic water bottles *per day* went into the trash; most bottled water is consumed away from home, with no convenient place for recycling. Carbon dioxide emitted just from transporting water from Fiji, Italy, and France to the United States equals about 9,700 tons—about the amount emitted by 1,700 cars on the road. Making plastic for the bottles burns up about 1.5 million barrels of oil each year (enough to power 100,000 cars). And there is virtually no health benefit; 40 percent of all bottled water IS tap water; Aquafina just admitted that it's mysterious "bottled at PWS " meant public water source! Even more important from health perspective: the public water supply is more strictly regulated by the EPA than bottled water is by the FDA, so you actually are safer drinking tap water

Until better alternatives become available, the best solution to reducing the impact of plastics on the environment is to promote recycling. Given the magnitude of this problem, we need a president who understands the urgent need to promote recycling. Plastics deteriorate but never decompose completely, but neither do glass, paper, or aluminum. Plastics make up 9.5 percent of our trash by weight compared to paper, which constitutes 38.9 percent. Glass and metals make up 13.9 percent by weight. Recycled plastics are used to make polymeric timbers for use in picnic tables, fences, and outdoor toys. Plastic from two-liter bottles is being spun into fiber for the production of carpet. We need to institute programs that encourage more recycling and minimize waste in production and use.

Separation of Church and State

One of the most important founding principles of our country rests on the idea that our government cannot impose one religion upon the people. McCain-Palin have other ideas, inconsistent with fundamental tenets of our Constitution. Palin's views, while extreme, accurately represent those of the Republican Party more generally. Examples abound. The Republican-appointed majority on the Supreme Court ruled in June 2007 (*Hein v. Freedom*

From Religion Foundation) that taxpayers may not challenge a Bush initiative to help religious organizations receive federal funds. At the heart of the case is a 1968 Supreme Court ruling that allowed taxpayers to sue government programs that promote religion; in that case a federal law that financed teaching and instructional materials in religious schools.

We have yet another attack on the constitutional protection that the government "shall make no law respecting an establishment of religion." The majority, including of course John Roberts and Samuel Alito appointed by Bush, said that taxpayers cannot challenge an executive branch program, arguing that the 1968 ruling covered only programs funded by congressional appropriation. Dissenting justices, including David Hackett Souter, maintained that position was absurd, saying the 1968 ruling draws no such line, and the logic of the majority has no basis in either precedent or logic. In shocking disregard for the Constitution, Bush advocated for new federal guidelines in 2003 that "push the envelope" on religion in public schools, well beyond what has traditionally been allowed by U.S. courts. The rules allow for and encourage "student-initiated" prayer and religious speech at public school events.

The role of military chaplains has come under increased scrutiny due to a lawsuit that links Air Force Academy officials with efforts to target nonreligious personnel for religious conversion, with the support of the right-wing evangelical Christian group Focus on the Family. Senator McCain has "no problem with the Ten Commandments posted on the wall of every public place" without considering if the Exodus 20 or Deuteronomy 5 version should be used. Catholics use the latter while Protestants claim the former.

In addition to promoting one religion, and breeding religious intolerance by implying government approval for one belief, the Ten Commandments offer little moral guidance. The first four have nothing to do with morality and are simply self-promoting. The others advocate obvious behaviors that do not need to be posted. Whether posted in the Old Testament or not, all societies everywhere in the world agree that random killing is bad and that theft is to be discouraged. Displaying the big ten is simply an effort to promote religion in the public domain, pure and simple. Let's leave religion and belief in the home, where they belong. McCain believes religion has a proper role in government. He apparently is not familiar with, or had disdain for, the founding documents of the country.

Foreign Assistance

Religious influence extends deeply into U.S. foreign policy. Reversing policy of the Clinton administration and reinstituting Reagan's Mexico City Policy, under the Bush administration the United States again terminated funding for any overseas organization that even discusses abortion with its patients. As a consequence, thousands of women are denied access to facilities that provide family planning and reproductive health services, including cervical screening and childhood immunization. In Latin America and Africa,

Roman Catholic bishops officially objected to the use of condoms, instead recommending abstinence to prevent AIDS. The bishops steadfastly held this view even in sub-Saharan Africa, where 26 million people are infected with AIDS, and more than 3 million more new infections occur each year. In Zambia, nearly 20 percent of the adult population is infected. Still, the bishops loyally follow the pope's mandate.

But a rapidly spreading AIDS epidemic is certainly not the only consequence of religious morality imposed on the question of family planning. Unwanted pregnancies in poor countries condemn women to an unrelenting cycle of poverty. Only when women gain control over their reproductive destiny and have access to education can the cycle be broken. But the church, with a concerted campaign against condom distribution, actively seeks to prevent women from gaining such control. This policy contributes directly to the suffering of millions of people relegated to hunger, disease, and illiteracy. The war against contraception, without concern for short-term suffering and the long-term consequences for human survival, is another sign that religious morality is deeply and tragically flawed.

Supreme Court Nominations

The next president will shape the course of American society for the next half-century through his appointments to the Supreme Court. Already we are seeing the impact of a sharp swing to the right. In June 2008, by a five-to-four vote, the Supreme Court overturned 230 years of precedent to accommodate the extreme agenda of the far right. Until this year, all previous courts have interpreted the amendment to protect the "right of the people of each of the several states to maintain a well-regulated militia" to mean just what is stated. But John Roberts, Antonin Scalia, and his cabal of radical activist jurists decided that a "well-regulated militia" meant "individuals" in a remarkable convolution of the English-language. Of course, Bush said the ruling was historic and supported the view long held by Republicans.

This latest turn of events should not be surprising given the Supreme Court's interference in the 2000 presidential election. What many Americans do not know is that John Roberts, who Bush later appointed as the chief justice of the Supreme Court, played a crucial role in preventing Al Gore from claiming his rightful victory. Only the most naive among us would view his role in Florida and his subsequent appointment as coincidental. Let's be clear: Roberts was rewarded for his partisan service by being appointed to the Supreme Court, where he now rules consistently in favor of the president he helped install in a judicial coup d'état.

Sex Scandals

The GOP is truly the Gay Old Party, and not the happy kind. The party that falsely prides itself on family values has been corrupted by a never-ending string of sex scandals. U.S. representative Mark Foley likes male pages, and urged one to "get a ruler and measure it for me." The venerable Ted Haggard, at the time the head of the National Association of Evangelicals, was accused of paying male prostitutes for sex while using crystal meth. This is the man who held weekly meetings with Bush, teaching the president that homosexuality is an abomination. U.S. senator Larry Craig was charged with soliciting sex in an airport bathroom. What made that interesting was his loud opposition to gay marriage. Bob Allen, a Republican congressman in the Florida House of Representatives, was charged with paying an undercover cop $20 for the pleasure of giving the officer oral sex. This act of illicit love was in bright contrast to his active sponsorship of anti-gay legislation. Glen Murphy Jr., while national chairman of the Young Republicans, allegedly got some young Republicans drunk and then decided to practice some oral sex on the inebriated up-and-comers. Republican state representative Richard Curtis from Spokane, Washington, was involved in a gay sex scandal. Donald Fleischman, chairman of the Republican Party in Brown County in Green Bay, Wisconsin, was ensnared in his own scandal of homosexual yearnings.

This list is by no means comprehensive, nor do these activities include the more than four thousand priests who have faced sex abuse charges in the past fifty years, involving more than ten thousand kids, mostly boys. But somehow the Republicans have painted Democrats as a threat to family values and the party of immorality. Amazing.

Family Values

In *What's the Matter with Kansas*, author and historian Thomas Frank explains how GOP members get elected using hot-button social issues, then ignore those issues to pursue economic policies that hurt the very people who elected them. This the upcoming presidential election removes any doubt about that thesis. Assume for just a moment that the Democratic nominee had an unwed teenage daughter pregnant at the age of seventeen. The response and attacks from the GOP would be predictable: Democrats do not share America's values, do not support the nuclear family, are immoral, and promote promiscuity. Only a Republican can represent the core values held by decent Americans.

But because the girl, Palin's daughter, happens to be the daughter of a Republican, the response is radically different. "All families have difficulties." One pundit said the issue just showed that Palin was human. Another piously claimed that the pregnancy showed that Palin had strong moral character because she was sticking with her daughter and the pregnant teen was, after all, marrying the father. Where is the moral outrage? Nowhere to be seen, because such moral outrage is not real. McCain and the Republicans simply use these issues, as Frank so clearly explains, as a political tool. The hypocrisy is so astonishing as to be almost worthy of awe.

Scandals The list of scandals in the Republican Party is long and impressive in scope, again belying any commitment to moral values. The past eight years have seen scandals in finance, gay sex, influence peddling, war preparation, treatment of returning vets, firing of U.S. attorneys, revealing the name of an active undercover CIA agent then lying under oath about it, civilian contractors, torture, illegal wire tapping, disaster response, illegal surveillance of financial transactions, rendition of Canadian and European citizens and arrest of Americans deprived of habeas corpus, military contracting bribes, interfering with family decisions in the Terri Schiavo case, failure to prevent 9/11 in the face of explicit warnings, cronyism and installing grossly inappropriate personnel in key positions, appointing Harriet Miers to the Supreme Court, taking cronyism to new heights, preventing the press from photographing coffins of Americans killed in Iraq, Abu Ghraib, mismanagement of Fannie Mae and Freddie Mac, indifference to Darfur, voter suppression on a massive scale, Antonio Scalia's refusal—after spending two days duck hunting with Cheney—to recuse himself from a Cheney appeal to keep Cheney's energy policy meetings secret. Some websites now report over three hundred major Republican scandals. This is the tradition to be carried on by McCain-Palin.

Second Amendment

The National Rifle Association (NRA) is coming to the rescue for all those living in fear that criminals are lurking behind every tree in our national parks. With Republican support, the NRA wants to allow national park visitors to carry concealed hand guns, not to mention loaded shotguns and rifles. Ronald Reagan was simply not conservative enough for these folks; the current rules they seek to change were implemented by the hero of the right. Reagan imposed rules that only allowed unloaded guns secured in a trunk or truck bed to pass through the park, with the idea of allowing hunters to travel to hunting grounds outside the park.

NRA lobbyist Chris Cox claims that families need loaded handguns to for protection while enjoying nature's bounty. What Cox fails to appreciate is that the lowest crime rates in the United State are found in our national parks. Introducing loaded guns will have no impact other than to create a new threat to visitors, officials, and unsuspecting wildlife like killer raccoons and vicious squirrels. The NRA is pushing this silly idea to take advantage of momentum created by the right-wing Supreme Court and the recent ruling on handguns in Washington, DC, applying the Second Amendment to individuals.

The Sarah Palin Problem

Who is Sarah Palin? Seemingly out of nowhere, Americans must decide whether a first-term governor of one of the smallest-population states in the country is qualified to be president of the United States of America. With a seventy-two-year-old running on the top of the ticket, what does the American electorate need to know about the first female vice-presidential candidate put forward by the Republican Party? Is she qualified? And what does it say about the judgment of Senator McCain that he picked her, after a fifteen-minute conversation, over many other self-evidently better-qualified individuals? The level of cynicism displayed in this Republican campaign, with party members faced with having to distance themselves from the most unpopular president in modern history, is stunning.

• Bridge to Nowhere but Lies

In her mocking, sarcastic, vice-presidential acceptance speech, and in every speech thereafter, Palin robotically repeats the obnoxious line that she "told Congress 'thanks but no thanks' on that bridge to nowhere."

The problem is that the claim is absolutely false. The infamous bridge was planned for the city of Ketchikan, and officials there confirm that Palin supported the bridge during her run for governor. During that campaign, Mayor Bob Weinstein claims that Palin went as far as saying she was insulted by the term "bridge to nowhere" in the press. Palin's support for the bridge cannot be disputed. In an interview with the *Anchorage Daily News* on October 22, 2006, a reporter asked Palin if she "would continue state funding for the proposed Knik Arm and Gravina Island bridges?" Her response was, "Yes. I would like to see Alaska's infrastructure projects built sooner rather than later. The window is now—while our congressional delegation is in a strong position to assist."

The bridge created a tempest of protests because the span linked Ketchikan to sparsely populated Gravina Island, hardly in need of the bridge. In campaign rallies, Palin told Ketchikan residents that she felt their pain when others called the city "nowhere" ignoring the obvious reference to Gravina Island. When the $223 million earmark became public, the bridge became the poster child of out of control pork-barrel spending. What was lost in the hyperbole was that the bridge was not meant to benefit the few dozen residents of Gravina Island, but was designed as a link to Ketchikan's airport, located on the island. Finger to the wind, Palin eventually backed away from supporting the structure.

Her lies did not end there. In nasally repeating the "thanks but no thanks" line, Palin implied clearly that she gave the money back. That is what "no thanks" means. Not so. Even after Congress removed the earmark, Alaska received the equivalent amount in the form of transportation dollars. Alaska was allowed to use the funds at the state's discretion.

• Firing While Hiring a Government Chef

Since adherence to the truth was not a requirement for anything in Palin's acceptance speech, she lied as well about firing the governor's chef. This was not a slip of the tongue in one speech. She repeated the line as robotically as she did the lie about the bridge to nowhere. At a rally in Colorado Springs she told the crowd, "And you may have heard, we did lay off the governor's personal chef. Though I do admit with that one, my kids aren't starving, but they sure do miss her." In fact, she did not fire the chef, who was simply reassigned to cook at the state legislature, largely because Palin spent so little time in the capital.

• Fiscal Irresponsibility in State Government

Lying comes easy to Palin, and this is evident in her absurd claim to be a responsible fiscal conservative. The town of Wasilla, Alaska, had a balanced budget when Palin became its mayor; the town was burdened by a debt of $22 million when she left office. Much of the debt came from Palin's support for a $15 million multiuse sports complex. Sadly, she built on a plot of land to which the city did not have clear title, giving lawyers more than seven years of income through continuing litigation. Palin did not spend to install a badly needed sewage treatment plant. Nevertheless, government spending increased more than 33 percent during her six-year tenure. Much of that was funded through an increase in sales tax.

This philosophy of spending and borrowing followed Palin to the governor's mansion or, more accurately, to her house for which she submitted per-diem reimbursements. Alaska ranks as number one among the fifty states in taxes per resident. That dubious distinction means that each resident suffers under a tax burden that is nearly two and a half times that of the national average.

• Minimum Qualifications to Govern

Austin, Texas, has a population greater than the entire state of Alaska. Does that mean the mayor is qualified to be president? Karl Rove clearly believes not, arguing that being mayor and governor are insufficient qualifiers to be president. At one point in the election, Governor Tim Kaine was on Obama's short list for vice president. Kaine is governor of Virginia, and previously served as mayor of Richmond, Virginia, which has a population of over 200,000. On August 10, before Palin was selected as McCain's vice-presidential choice, Rove said the following in an August 10 discussion about Kaine: "He's been a governor for three years, he was mayor of the one-hundred-fifth-largest city in America, now again, with all due respect to Richmond, Virginia, it's smaller than Chula Vista, California; Aurora, Colorado; Mesa or Gilbert, Arizona; North Las Vegas or Henderson, Nevada; it's not a big town. *So if you were to pick Governor Kaine it would be an intensely political choice where it said, 'You know what, I'm really not first and foremost concerned with is this person capable of being President of the United States . . .'"* (emphasis added).

But truth, reality, and honor have no place in Rove's world. So when McCain chose Palin, Rove completely reversed himself, with no shame, and said, "She's a populist, she's an economic and a social conservative, she's a reformer, she's a former mayor, she was the mayor, I think, of the second largest city in Alaska before she ran for governor . . ." As often is the case, Rove was wrong. Cities in Alaska in order of size and population are Anchorage, Fairbanks, Juneau, Ketchikan . . . Wasilla is not even close to second largest. Rove simply never lets facts stand in his way.

Rove is impressed by Palin's foreign policy experience: she can see Russia off in the distance. Yes, that constitutes her entire portfolio. For good reason the GOP is afraid to let her out alone. Palin did not give an interview to the press for more than two weeks after her nomination, a communications gap for the vice-presidential candidate never before seen in modern American politics. The reason for that became clear when she finally sat down for an interview with Charlie Gibson. She was clueless about the Bush doctrine and then pretended she knew when confronted. When asked if she had met any foreign leaders, she said no but then went on to claim that is the case for most vice-presidential candidates. Again, just plain wrong. Every vice-presidential candidate since the Eisenhower administration has met with foreign leaders prior to being nominated. Since 1933 when Franklin D. Roosevelt chose John Nance Garner, every candidate for the vice presidency has had foreign policy experience that included meeting foreign leaders. Palin's answer to the question reveals an ignorance of American history as well as an easy willingness to manipulate the truth.

A Woman's Right to Choose

Palin wants the government, the same one she decries endlessly, to prevent a woman from choosing her own reproductive destiny. Palin actually said she would oppose abortion even in the case of rape, even if the victim were her daughter. Even among abortion opponents, her views are extreme. In spite of quite obvious evidence that teaching abstinence does not work, particularly within her own family, Palin opposes sex education. She also slashed funding for programs that supported pregnant teens. Palin made women pay for rape kits in Wasilla. Apparently the governor wants girls to suffer. Palin's policies and actions are unambiguously driven by her religion, with wanton disregard for constitutional niceties like separation of church and state.

Federal Debts and Deficits

The biggest lie ever perpetuated by the Republican media machine is the notion that the GOP is the party of tax relief and fiscal responsibility. Ronald Reagan, hero of the right, taxed the American people at unprecedented levels. His Tax Equity and Fiscal Responsibility Act of 1982, TEFRA, was the largest tax increase in American history, designed to raise $214.1 billion over five years. The largest debts accumulated under conservative Republicans. The debt created by Reagan's budgets as submitted, not as altered by

Democrats, tripled to an amount that exceeded at that time the combined total of all previous debts since the founding of our country. That was not a fluke of just one president. In less than eight years, the Bush administration has burdened the United States with a debt now greater than 9.6 trillion dollars. The largest operating deficits have all been under Republicans, including a $400 billion debt in 2008. Expect more of the same discredited economic policies with McCain-Palin.

Cronyism and Corruption

Republicans denigrate government, but do not hesitate to pillage public coffers when in office. No political party has a greater tradition of giving jobs to friends with no regard to qualifications. Remember "You're doing a great job, Brownie" after Katrina? The Bush administration is populated by more than 150 graduates of Pat Robertson's Regent Law School. The most recent poster child for this cronyism is Monica Goodling, who resigned in disgrace in the wake of the scandalous firings of U.S. attorneys general. Goodling was hired to supervise U.S. prosecutors, even though she herself had virtually no prosecutorial experience. Her primary qualification was that she admired George Bush. Such disregard for common sense and job qualifications is the first step to corruption because people incompetent to serve often bring disdain for the position to the job. Hence we witnessed the unprecedented politicization of the Justice Department under Bush, who corrupted the office given the responsibility to enforce the nation's laws without regard to politics.

McCain-Palin will continue this sad tradition. McCain claims the mantle of maverick, but he is nothing but more of the same. Americans seem to have conveniently forgotten John McCain's role in the Keating Five scandal and his role in helping friends by abusing his power and influence. Yes, McCain was eventually cleared of violating the law, but he was reprimanded for "exercising poor judgment" in providing assistance to Charles Keating in the savings and loan crisis. This matters because that scandal in 1989 is reminiscent of the mortgage crisis the country now faces, with record foreclosures and failures of Freddie Mac and Fannie Mae. McCain is not the man to lead us back to fiscal sanity.

Nor is Palin anything like the reformer she proclaims to be. In her short tenure as governor, she has taken cronyism to new heights. Being a friend of Palin was often the only obvious qualification to secure a job in her administration. Deborah Richter, a close Palin friend and political fund-raiser, was appointed as director of the Permanent Fund Dividend Division to hand out oil dividend checks to Alaskan residents. Palin chose her close friend Talis Colberg to be attorney general, even though Colberg's experience was restricted to insurance law. Friendship rather than qualification was used to select leaders of two of the most important jobs in Alaskan government. Palin's record does not bode well in the wake of the Alberto Gonzales in the Bush Justice Department.

A Woman's Right to Choose

A woman's right to choose her own reproductive destiny hangs by one Supreme Court justice vote. The next president will likely be able to nominate at least two. This fact alone should be enough to induce the majority of voters who believe in a modern, reasonable approach to choice to support Obama in this election. A McCain-Palin presidency would enable a radical agenda not supported by the majority of the population, women and men included. As Obama so eloquently noted in his acceptance speech at the Democratic National Convention, we may disagree on reproductive freedom, but we can agree to reduce the number of abortions in this country. Abortion is an invasive surgical technique, physically and psychologically traumatic, expensive, and potentially dangerous. Part of the adult responsibility commensurate with having an active sex life is prudent and careful use of contraception. Unwanted pregnancy should be exceptional rather than routine.

Education is the most effective tool to reduce the number of abortions. But a woman's right to determine her own reproductive destiny should never be subject to the whims of old white men sitting in state capitals or in the U.S. Congress or on the bench of the Supreme Court. Nevertheless, the religious right is now firmly established in power in all branches of the federal government, and in the majority of state capitals. The result has real consequences in daily life, affecting intimate and personal aspects of our lives such as sex and reproductive choice. A woman's right to choose has never been more threatened.

Fetal rights are the latest weapon in the arsenal of the anti-choice movement to limit a woman's rights and to create a separate legal identity for mother and fetus. Americans on both sides of the debate hold inconsistent views that are swept under the rug. Advocates for and against speak in euphemisms instead of tackling the issues honestly and head on. If abortion is murder, how can we make any exceptions for rape and incest? Yet the vast majority of Americans favor such exceptions.

The idea that life begins at conception is deeply flawed. True, a fetus has the potential to become human—if it successfully implants in the uterus, is not rejected by the mother's immune system, has no fatal chromosomal abnormalities, and the mother herself does not die before giving birth. But an unfertilized egg also has the potential to become human, every bit as much as a fetus, every bit as dependent on a series of contingent events; it just needs to be fertilized first. Each individual sperm has the potential to become human; it just needs to fertilize an egg. An egg, a sperm, and an embryo all have the *potential* to become human, and all must be treated equally. Conferring special rights to a fertilized egg is arbitrary and the result of religious morality imposed on society. If you believe that life begins at conception, then a woman is committing murder every time she ovulates and a man is commuting millions of murders with each ejaculation. Despite sensational appeals to emotion, early-term abortions are removing tissue that has not yet developed into human form. In the absence of a central nervous system, the embryo is incapable of any sensation. Until a brain has developed a functioning cortex, the embryo has no ability to form any conscious thought. About eight weeks after fertilization, the first detectable brain waves can be recorded, but the brain is not nearly fully formed and the cerebral cortex is poorly distinguished. Before eight weeks, in the absence of any brain function, the growing embryo is little different in its human potential from a fertilized egg.

Later stages of growth do not offer a sign as clear as brain development, but the fetus itself provides another point of determination, although one involving a higher emotional and ethical cost in the hierarchy of decision making: before and after the fetus is capable of living outside the womb, without invasive medical intervention, still fully dependent on the mother's body to support life. Before that point of development, the line from potential to actual human has not been crossed. After that point, abortion becomes problematic and should be severely restricted.

Finally, we must question the consistency of the Republican position—a party that has long held the belief that a smaller government is better is perfectly willing to use government to stand in for the personal moral and ethical values of private citizens.

First Amendment First to Go

The evangelical religious right continues to invade and pervert American politics. Let's be clear about a point that cannot be disputed: the Constitution of the United States nowhere mentions God or Christianity. That is a fact. Yet religion so dominates American life and has infiltrated our educational system so deeply that even basic facts about our government and history are seen through the distorted lens of religion. Faith has triumphed over reason and fact.

According to the State of the First Amendment 2007 national survey released on September 12 by the First Amendment Center, we see the following frightening statistics: more than 65 percent of Americans believe that the nation's founders intended the United States to be a Christian nation; 55 percent believe that the Constitution establishes a Christian nation; 74 percent of Republicans endorse the notion of a constitutional provision for a Christian nation; 50 percent of Democrats and 47 percent of independent voters agree. Just 56 percent believe that the freedom to worship as one chooses extends to all religious groups, regardless of how extreme, down sixteen points from 72 percent in 2000. What we see in these alarming numbers is a precipitous degradation of our basic freedoms, willingly ceded by Americans blinded by faith.

This perspective has real consequences. Faith-based reasoning is why we are now mired in Iraq. With faith, one is free to ignore facts; one can simply believe, and that is enough. One is free to fabricate as long as one believes. When your instructions come directly from God, why examine facts on the ground? The results of this approach are obvious and catastrophic. We can and must do better. We must return to the roots of our founding fathers, recapture reason as the basis for our foreign policy decisions, and recommit to secular laws creating domestic policies that can be sustained realistically.

We are not a Christian nation; we are a nation of Jews, Catholics, Protestants, Muslims, and secularists. We are a nation of laws and logic. Any move away from that foundation is a grave threat to our very existence. The marriage of theology and ideology is a dangerous union, inherently blind to reason.

Scientific Advisory Committees

In March 2007, the Fish and Wildlife Service, part of the Department of the Interior, did something astounding in preparation for an international meeting in Norway on conserving arctic animals: the two scientists representing the service were prevented from speaking about or responding to questions about climate change! A spokesperson said that climate change was not an agenda item! A truly absurd claim because a primary concern of the meeting was how melting ice sheets would affect arctic life.

This is not an isolated event: Michael Griffin, head of the National Aeronautics and Space Administration (NASA), says that climate change is not a problem we need to wrestle with. NASA has consistently prevented its scientists from discussing climate change, and, in particular, has repeatedly tried to muzzle one of their chief scientists, Jim Hansen. This is how Bush handles facts he does not like. President Bush's administration deleted the following from the congressional testimony of Julia Gerberding, director of the Centers for Disease Control and Prevention: "Scientific evidence supports the view that the climate is changing."

More than sixty prominent scientists, including twenty Nobel laureates, have signed a declaration stating "that the scope and scale of the manipulation, suppression, and misrepresentation of science by the Bush Administration is unprecedented." More than four thousand scientists, including forty-eight Nobel laureates and 127 members of the National Academy of Science, have signed a statement declaring, "Across a broad range of policy areas, the administration has undermined the quality and independence of the scientific advisory system and the morale of the government's outstanding scientific personnel."

The list of examples of such attacks on reason, and subversion of science, is long and disturbing. A few of the worst cases are described below.

• In September, 2002, the administration removed a section on climate change from the EPA's annual air pollution report, although that section had been an integral part of the report for the five preceding years. In June 2003, the White House tried to change EPA's draft Report on the Environment, hoping to delete reference to a National Academy of Science report concluding that human activity is contributing to climate change. The White House objected to EPA's draft language, widely accepted in the scientific community, that "climate change has global consequences for human health and the environment."

• The administration tried to suppress the use of a well-established thousand-year temperature record, instead substituting an analysis that supported the administration's position.

• The White House Council on Environmental Quality censored, and then ceased publication of, a USDA brochure recommending steps that farmers could take to reduce greenhouse gas emissions.

• After ten years of study, and independent peer review by the National Academy of Science, a scientific team issued final findings on species management along the Missouri River, listing actions that were to take effect in 2003. But Bush stepped in, inserted a new team, and revised the biological conclusions from the ten-year study, with conclusions suitable to the White House.

• President Bush overruled a $12 million science-based management plan for old-growth forest in eleven national parks; he did so with a "review team" consisting largely of nonscientists with no forestry expertise; plan changes included doubling or tripling the harvest and relaxing standards for cattle grazing

• Tightening standards for lead pollution and poisoning were avoided by the Bush administration by making last-minute changes to an expert panel, packing the committee with industry-friendly staff and dismissing world-renowned experts on lead.

• In an extraordinary move, the FDA disapproved over-the-counter sales of Plan B (a "morning after" contraceptive) by overriding the agency's scientists; the Government Accounting Office later concluded that the FDA "diverged sharply from usual agency procedures."

• The White House has attacked science so severely that even the states are fighting back. A coalition of twelve states sued the EPA to block the Bush administration from relaxing key elements of the Clean Air Act

• On December 21, 2005, the EPA proposed air quality standards for fine particulate matter that were weaker than even the most generous standards proposed by the Clean Air Science Advisory Committee

• On March 17, 2006, a three-judge panel of the U.S. Court of Appeals in Washington, DC, overturned Bush's "routine maintenance" rule, which exempted one thousand of air polluters from regulation.

• The White House is not satisfied with attacking clean air; they now have water in their crosshairs, taking actions that will virtually dismantle the Clean Water Act passed thirty years ago and now considered one of the most successful environmental laws ever enacted

• On February 16, 2006, the Bush White House proposed lowering drinking-water quality standards for poor and rural communities.

Creation Science

In spite of the unprecedented success of the theory of evolution in explaining the living world, in spite of the fact that the theory of evolution is one of the greatest triumphs of science, creationism and intelligent design have crept into mainstream of American thought and into public school curricula in several states. A poll conducted by the People for the American Way Foundation showed that only 37 percent of the population believes evolution should be taught and creationism excluded. A Gallup poll in 2001 showed that 40 percent of Catholics in the United States believe that God created human life in the past ten thousand years. These grim statistics would have surprised even Pope John Paul II, who in 1996 reaffirmed that the church accepted evolution, although with some strong caveats, and about five hundred years late.

If we fail to change course and overcome this shameful level of collective ignorance about creation, we will soon be forced to teach the stork theory of reproduction in schools as an alternative to the theory of sexual reproduction. But why stop there? We could soon be teaching that the sun orbits around the earth as the Bible claims, as an alternative to the theory of orbital mechanics. Only by understanding the fundamentals of evolution can we put an end to the madness of creationism and intelligent design and regain a rational sense of our place in the universe.

Attempts to reconcile religion and science are futile and unproductive. Science searches for mechanisms and the answer to how the universe functions. Religion seeks meaning and the answer to why the world is as we know it. Science and religion can never be brought under one roof without sacrificing intellectual honesty. The two seek different answers to separate questions using fundamentally incompatible methods. Nothing can bring the two together. Yet the effort to reconcile continues. The latest example is the idea put forth by Richard Colling at Olivet Nazarene University, who writes that God "cares enough about creation to harness even the forces of (Darwinian) randomness." God used Darwin to implement his will! The bizarre logic behind this idea is that the facts of evolution do not preclude the existence of God. In fact, evolution and natural selection do indeed preclude the existence of God, according to the Bible itself. We are told in Genesis that all life, everything that ever existed on earth, was created in six days. Evolution proves that wrong. The fossil record proves that wrong. Evolution in a Petri dish proves that wrong.

The fundamental randomness of evolution through natural selection creates a terminal problem for any hand of God. If God is all knowing, He knew everything from the beginning of the universe, including every animal that would ever exist. That would preclude any animals evolving from random processes, since a truly random God could not then have known about them beforehand, meaning He would not be all knowing. Yet if He in fact did know about all animals past and future, then that is not evolution, which is random by definition.

Natural selection and evolution are inherently incompatible with the existence of God. The two cannot coexist.

But religion has taken such a stranglehold on American thought that believers will go through extreme contortions to incorporate the indisputable facts of evolution into a belief system fully undermined by the mechanisms of natural selection. The rest of the world understands that evolution is the most thoroughly tested, documented, proven scientific fact ever put forth. Evolution is a proven reality no less than the fact that the atom is a building block of nature. To debate evolution is to question that the earth is round or that DNA forms the basis of the genetic code. Next, under Palin, we will be promoting the stork theory of reproduction. To question the reality of evolution is no less absurd.

Yet animosity toward evolution, rather than abating in the face of greater human knowledge, is being further attacked in an ocean of ignorance. The new Creation Museum in Kentucky proudly states its purpose as countering "evolutionary natural history museums that turn countless minds against Christ and Scripture." That we are still having this discussion is sad testament to the serious degradation of our public school system. We are failing to teach our population even the most basic aspects of elementary science in an era where science and technology are ever more critical to our national security. Unless we conquer this growing threat of scientific illiteracy, our nation is doomed. We will become a second-rate nation lagging behind in stem cell research, high-energy physics, biology, and medicine. Our infrastructure will continue to crumble with no progress in materials science.

We will be poorly equipped to fight the growing technological prowess of our adversaries. We must stop this ridiculous debate about evolution and get on with the business of protecting ourselves in the twenty-first century.

Sanctity of Life

The phrase "sanctity of life" is used by opponents of abortion to indicate a pious regard for all things living. But nothing could be further from the truth because opponents of abortion are almost universally in favor of the death penalty. Support for state-sanctioned death is as strong as ever among conservative Republicans, despite the fact that DNA evidence has exonerated 172 prisoners death row. Abortion foes do not view life as sacred; only some life and, certainly, only human life. But not all human life: killing in war is justified, as is lethal injection for convicted criminals. Killing an intruder is acceptable.

Cows are alive, but killing them for food is not questioned. Hunting big game for sport is just fine. But cows and big game are alive, so the unctuous appeal to the sanctity of life is absurd. What conservative Republicans mean is that some forms of life, which only they have the right to define, are sacred. Others can be disregarded like trash. Just as Republicans have no unique claim to patriotism or family values, they have no special status in defining life as sacred. This country desperately needs, and will have in Obama, a president who respects the views of others, who governs inclusively, and who will stop using wedge issues to divide and conquer.

Banana Republic

The Democracy that Can't Shoot or Vote Straight

Hanging chads are not our only problem. For a country that represents itself as a leading example of democracy, we have failed to provide our citizenry with a viable means to vote. While we live in the age of computers, the 2008 election will mark a milestone from the Stone Age: more Americans will cast their vote on paper than in any other election in our nation's history. After the Florida fiasco in 2000, the government put in place a $3 billion plan to upgrade voting technology. We can go to the moon, but . . .

The result? Concerns about hacking, unscrupulous manufacturers with ties to the Republican Party, and never-ending technical failures mean that tens of thousands of touch-screen machines now serve as unwanted paperweights in warehouses across the country. Poor counties will now need to set aside resources to pay for printing ballots, an expense once thought to be off the books. Voters will be confused anew by inconsistent ballot formats. Idaho still uses punch cards like those leading to chad-hunting in Florida. Many states will require voters to fill in little ovals to mark their votes.

This again is a case of bad resource allocation. We cannot even put in place the basic mechanics of democracy.

We're back to being a banana republic. The governor of the state in dispute is the brother of the victorious candidate. The secretary of State overseeing the recount process was an unabashedly partisan Republican. Supreme Court justices appointed by Republicans voted to install the Republican candidate in office (against their long-standing views on states' rights). The newly appointed (but not elected) president then appointed his lead attorney who argued his case before the Supreme Court as the chief justice of the Supreme Court! We couldn't even make this stuff up; and now we are setting ourselves up for a repeat. Why would the Republicans want to solve a "problem" that allowed them to assume the presidency even after losing the election.

So where do we go from here?

This book has one simple purpose: to give concerned citizens information and talking points to help you make the case for Obama-Biden and against McCain-Palin. It was written in less than forty-eight hours out of a passionate concern for the future of our country, drawn from a deep love of this country and the natural world we all inhabit. Together with my publisher, we have put together a website, www.votetosavetheplanet.com, where we invite all readers to join in the discussion about our future and the election to come.

Recommended Resources

Here are some resources to help us all **Vote! to Save the Planet.**

Books

American Theocracy: The Peril and Politics of Radical Religion, Oil, and Borrowed Money in the 21st Century
Author: Kevin Phillips
$26.95
ISBN-10: 067003486X

Angler: The Cheney Vice Presidency
Author: Barton Gellman
$27.95
ISBN-13: 978-1594201868

The Assault on Reason
Author: Al Gore
$16.00
ISBN-13: 978-0143113621

The Audacity of Hope
Author: Barack Obama
Price: $7.99
ISBN 10: 0307455874

Change We Can Believe In: Barack Obama's Plan to Renew America's Promise
Author: Barack Obama
$13.95
ISBN-13: 978-0307460455

The Conscience of a Liberal
Author: Paul Krugman
$25.95
ISBN-13: 978-039306069

*The Dark Side: The Inside Story of How The War on Terror
Turned into a War on American Ideals*
Author: Jane Mayer
$27.50
ISBN-13: 978-0385526395

Dead Certain: The Presidency of George W. Bush
Author: Robert Draper
$15.00
ISBN-13: 978-0743277297

*Democrats Soul: A Tried-and-True View of Everything
Blue*
Author: Compilation
$9.95
ISBN-13: 978-0757306754

The End of America: Letter of Warning to a Young Patriot
Author: Naomi Wolf
$13.95
ISBN-13: 978-1933392790

*Energy Victory: Winning the War on Terror by Breaking
Free of Oil*
Author: Robert Zubrin
$25.95
ISBN-13: 978-1591025917

*The Future of Freedom: Illiberal Democracy at Home
and Abroad*
Author: Fareed Zakaria
$15.95
ISBN-13: 978-0393331523

Hot, Flat, and Crowded: Why We Need a Green Revolution—and How It Can Renew America
Author: Thomas L. Friedman
$27.95
ISBN-13: 978-0374166854

Living History
Author: Hillary Rodham Clinton
$16.00
ISBN-13: 978-0743222259

Marching Toward Hell: America and Islam After Iraq
Author: Michael Scheuer
$27.00
ISBN-13: 978-0743299695

Mike's Election Guide 2008
Author: Michael Moore
$13.99
ISBN-13: 978-0446546270

Obama: From Promise to Power
Author: David Mendell
$7.99
ISBN-13: 978-0061736667

The Obama Nation
Author: Jerome R. Corsi
$28.00
ISBN-10: 1416598065

Obamanomics: How Bottom-Up Economic Prosperity Will Replace Trickle-Down Economics
Author: John R. Talbott
$25.95
ISBN-13: 978-1583228654

The Political Brain: The Role of Emotion in Deciding the Fate of the Nation
Author: Drew Westen
$15.95
ISBN-13: 978-1586485733

The Political Mind: Why You Can't Understand 21st-Century American Politics with an 18th-Century Brain
Author: George Lakoff
$25.95
ISBN-13: 978-0670019274

Promises to Keep: On Life and Politics
Author: Senator Joseph Biden
$15.00
ISBN-13: 978-0812976212

Renew America
Author: Thomas L. Friedman
$27.95
ISBN-13: 978-0374166854

The Shock Doctrine: The Rise of Disaster Capitalism
Author: Naomi Klein
$16.00
ISBN-13: 978-0312427993

Standing Up to the Madness: Ordinary Heroes in Extraordinary Times
Author: Amy Goodman and David Goodman
$23.95
ISBN-13: 978-1401322885

A Time to Fight: Reclaiming a Fair and Just America
Author: Jim Webb
$24.95
ISBN-13: 978-0767928359

Third Term: Why George W. Bush (Hearts) John McCain
Author: Paul Begala
$15.00
ISBN-13: 978-1439102138

*Who Killed the Constitution?: The Fate of American
Liberty from World War I to George W. Bush*
Author: Thomas E. Woods Jr. and Kevin R. C. Gutzman
$25.95
ISBN-13: 978-0307405753

*Why We're Liberals: A Political Handbook for Post-Bush
America*
Author: Eric Alterman
$25.00
ISBN-10: 0670018600

The Wrecking Crew: How Conservatives Rule
Author: Thomas Frank
$25.00
ISBN-13: 978-0805079883

*Your Government Failed You: Breaking the Cycle of
National Security Disasters*
Author: Richard A. Clarke
$25.95
ISBN-13: 978-0061474620

Websites and Blogs

Bare Naked Pundits
www.Barenakedpundits.com

Chelsea Green Press
www.Chelseagreen.com

Common Dreams
www.Commondreams.org

Conscious Communications
www.Consciouscomm.com

Daily Kos
www.Dailykos.com

Eventful: Demand Barack Obama
www.eventful.com/performers/P0-001-000000162-8/
demand?from_sticker=300x325_blueflag

Fire Dog Lake
www.Firedoglake.com

Future Majority
www.Futuremajority.com

Huffington Post
www.Huffingtonpost.com

Info Wars
www.Infowars.com

Instapundits
www.Instapundits.com

Liberal Oasis
www.Liberaloasis.com

The Nation
www.Thenation.com

Populist
www.Populist.com

Propagenda
www.Progagenda.com

Talking Points Memo
www.Talkingpointsmemo.com

Tompaine
www.Tompaine.com

Tree Hugger
www.Treehugger.com

The Vote Cast
www.Thevotecast.com

Magazines

American Prospect
www.Prospect.org

Boston Review
www.Bostonreview.net

CounterPunch
www.Counterpunch.org

In Motion
www.Inmotionmagazine.com

In These Times
www.Inthesetimes.com

Mother Jones
www.Motherjones.com

The Nation
www.Thenation.com

The Progressive
www.Progressive.org

Third Estate Sunday Review
www.Thirdestatesundayreview.blogspot.com

Utne Reader
www.Utne.com

Wired
www.Wired.com

Z Magazine
www.Zmag.org

Organizations and Foundations

Alternet
www.Alternet.org

American Civil Liberties Union
www.Aclu.org

Center for Constitutional Rights
www.Ccrjustice.org

Eat the State
www.Eatthestate.org

Electronic Frontier Foundation
www.Eff.org

Independent Media Center
www.Indymedia.org/

Left Turn
www.Leftturn.org

YPM—Youth Progressive Majority
www.Goypm.org

Websites and Organizations Dedicated to Voting Issues and Education

America Votes
www.Americavotes.org

BBYO
www.Bbyo.org

Civic Youth
www.Civicyouth.org

Close Up Foundation/First Vote
www.Closeup.org

College Democrats of America
www.Collegedems.com

Courage Campaign
www.Couragecampaign.org

Declare Yourself
www.Declareyourself.com

Donkaphant Film Festival
www.Donkaphant.com

DoSomething
www.Dosomething.org

Easy Voter Guide
www.Easyvoter.org/s2.html

18 in 08
www.18in08.com

18 to 35
www.18to35.org

Election Day: One Day to Make It Count
www.Electiondaythemovie.com

Generation Engage
www.Generationengage.org

Get in the Game
www.Gitg-vote.com

Kids Voting USA
www.Kidsvotingusa.org

League of Women Voters
www.Lwv.org

Mobilize.org
www.Mobilize.org

New Voters Project
www.Newvotersproject.org

The Politico
www.Politico.com

Presidential Classroom
www.Presidentialclassroom.org

Project Vote Smart
www.Votesmart.org

Punk Voter
www.Punkvoter.com/

Rock the Vote
www.Rockthevote.org

Save Voting
www.Savevoting.org

Smackdown Your Vote
www.Vote.wwe.com

Smart Voter
www.Smartvoter.org

Southwest Voter Registration Project
www.SVREP.org

The Student PIRGs
www.Studentpirgs.org

2020 Vision
www.2020vision.org

The White House Project: Vote, Run, Lead
www.Thewhitehouseproject.org/voterunlead/

Ur Votes Count
www.Urvotescount.com

USA.gov
www.Usa.gov

Vote 18
www.Vote18.org

Vote for America
www.Voteforamerica.org

Vote Hope: Obama in '08
www.Votehope2008.org

Vote411
www.Vote411.org

Voto Latino
www.Votolatino.org

Vote! to Save the Planet David Wilk, Jacquie Jordan, and Darice Fisher came up with the idea to create this book during a conversation about Jeff Schweitzer's great ideas and his forthcoming book, *Beyond Cosmic Dice*, which Jacquie Jordan Inc. will publish in 2009.

That was on September 12. Jeff was somehow able to write the first draft of *Vote! to Save the Planet* by September 15. Meanwhile, we had set a great project in motion, based on the central premise in this book: we need to do everything we possibly can to insure an Obama-Biden victory in November.

We know that time is short, but that is what motivated all of us. We hope that whoever reads this book will agree that it was worth the effort. Use this book or our website, www.votetosavetheplanet.com as a starting point for your own efforts to make positive change and make a difference.

Credits

David Wilk edited *Vote! to Save the Planet* and contributed some original writing; he also compiled the Resources section with the help of Emily-Rose Wagner.

David Burstein of 18in08.com gave us some great voting resources.

Gray Cutler copyedited every page, and David Kessler proofread every word, both contributing their good work in a very short time frame.

Barbara Aronica-Buck designed the excellent cover and interior of the book in less than forty-eight hours.

Ryan Waggoner and Ben Lew took Barbara's design and made it into our website, www.votetosavethe planet.com, also in less than forty-eight hours.

Jacquie Jordan and Darice Fisher worked long hours to put together all the pieces of the book and made contacts with political and media people all over the United States to get this project out into the world.

Adam Schmidt of DNAML, Inc., recognized that this book needed to be published electronically and volunteered his company's services to get it done.

Our wonderful sales team, Ruth Hook, Richard Re, and Tony Proe of The Empire Group supported us from the moment they heard about the book and got the word out to the book trade.

About the Author

Dr. Jeff Schweitzer is an internationally recognized authority in bridging science, conservation, development and ethics. He has been a guest speaker at dozens of international conferences in Asia, Russia, Europe and across the United States. He was Assistant Director for International Affairs in the Office of Science and Technology Policy in the Clinton-Gore administration.